TAMING THE TORNADO TUBE

50 Weird & Wacky Things You Can Do With a Tornado Tube

by Steve Spangler

Consulting Editors
Linda Baltich & Harriet Kinghorn

Illustrated by
Vickie Leigh Krudwig

Cover Photograph by
Steve Mohlenkamp

WREN Publishing
Englewood, Colorado

Published by WREN Publishing
WREN Publishing, a division of WREN Enterprises, Inc.
3145 West Monmouth Avenue
Englewood, Colorado 80110

We wish to thank the children and parents who have given their permission to include material in this book. Every effort has been made to acknowledge all of the contributors of activities. We regret any oversights that may have occurred and would be happy to rectify them in future printings.

Tornado Tube® is a registered trademark of Burnham and Associates, Inc., and is assigned U.S. Patent 4625780.

Illustrator: Vickie Leigh Krudwig
Consulting Editors: Linda Baltich, Harriet Kinghorn
Copy Editor: Nancy Reed
Cover Design: Tom Goellner

The publisher and the author have made every reasonable effort to ensure that the experiments and activities in this book are safe when conducted as instructed and with the proper adult supervision, but assumes no responsibility for any damage caused or sustained while performing the experiments and activities in this book.

Library of Congress Cataloging-in Publication Data

Spangler, Steve
    Taming the Tornado Tube, 50 Weird and Wacky Things You Can Do With a Tornado Tube / by Steve Spangler; illustrated by Vickie Leigh Krudwig.

        p.   cm.
Summary: Explanation of vortex action in nature and instructions for performing experiments and activities with soda bottles and the Tornado Tube connector.

ISBN   0-964-93530-9   Paper Text
          0-964-93531-7   Paper Text with Tornado Tube

Printed in the United States of America

10 9 8 7 6 5 4 3

A Million Thanks

The author wishes to thank the following people for their suggestions and contributions:

Kyp Henn from *Play 'N Learn Sales* who introduced me to Craig Burnham and created a need for this book,

Craig Burnham, the inventor of the *Tornado Tube®*, for his support and encouragement to write this book,

The Regis University *Hands-on Science Institute* staff and the teachers who shared their ideas and curriculum suggestions,

The children who attended the *1995 Summer Science Camp for Kids* at Regis University and shared their wit and creativity,

Dr. Jim Giulianelli, Professor of Chemistry at Regis University, whose enthusiasm and love of learning will never be forgotten,

Jeff Brooks, our faithful laboratory manager, who cleaned up the never ending mess and kept us in a sufficient supply of plastic soda bottles,

Bekye Dewey, Science Education Consultant from Fairfax Country Public Schools, for testing many of the demonstrations with her students,

Vickie Leigh Krudwig for her masterful illustrations, cover design, book layout, printing coordination, and her tireless dedication to finish the book,

Linda Baltich and Harriet Kinghorn for their wealth of ideas, technical research and writing,

Nancy Reed for her hours of editing, re-editing, and editing some more,

Mae, Lou, and Lisa Lamberson for overseeing multiple projects, offering warehouse space, and entertaining Shadow during all of those road trips,

Kitty and Bruce Spangler for teaching us that weird & wacky is good,

And, of course, my wife Renée for never being afraid to tackle any project, even if it means turning her kitchen into a laboratory and putting up with a husband who is always out in left field.

Dedication

Dedicated to Dr. Jim Giulianelli

Thanks for the endless hours of wonder, discovery,
exploration, and companionship.

You were a master science demonstrator,
an excellent teacher, and always a best friend.

You are greatly missed...

Table of Contents

Chapter 1

Chapter 2

Chapter 3

Chapter 4

Chapter 5

Chapter 6

Chapter 1

All About the Tornado Tube

What is a Tornado Tube?

It's quite simple. A *Tornado Tube* is a specially molded plastic tube that screws onto the top of a plastic soda bottle. It's designed to connect two soda bottles as shown in the illustration below. Before the bottles are connected with the *Tornado Tube*, one bottle is filled about half full with water. Connect the other bottle using the *Tornado Tube* and you're in business.

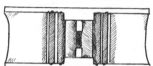

The Object of the Game

The object of the challenge is to cause all of the water in the top bottle to empty into the lower bottle as quickly as possible. Turn the bottles so that the water is in the top bottle and the *empty* bottle is on the bottom. Look closely. Is the bottom bottle really empty? No, in fact there's air in this bottle, and air occupies space. In order for the water to flow from the upper bottle into the lower bottle, the air in the lower bottle has to move to the upper bottle. Can you figure out how to do this?

As we'll learn later in this chapter, the inventor of the *Tornado Tube*, Craig Burnham, was faced with the same problem as a young boy. How do you get the water to flow from the upper bottle into the lower bottle? He became so frustrated with the problem that he eventually shook the bottles...and something unbelievable happened. In shaking the bottles, he actually swirled the water in a circular motion. The spinning water created what looked like a tornado in the bottle. It's actually called a *vortex*.

If you've ever seen a dust devil on a windy day or watched the water drain from the bathtub, you've seen a vortex. Because the middle of the vortex is hollow, the air from the lower bottle flows through the vortex into the upper bottle. At the same time the air is moving upward, the water flows downward into the lower bottle. The swirling action of the water is indeed the secret.

Swirling Water

About This Book

Some versions of this book are sold with a *Tornado Tube* attached to the upper left-hand corner. If you purchased the book without the accompanying *Tornado Tube*, we'll assume that you already own one of these toys. In any event, you'll need a *Tornado Tube* and some plastic soda bottles in order to conduct the experiments and activities in this book.

So, your first job is to start collecting 2-liter plastic soda bottles. Now, this does not mean that you're supposed to *empty* soda bottles, but rather *find* empty soda bottles. One place to find empty bottles is the recycling bin at a grocery store or recycling station. While the smaller 1-liter bottles are gaining popularity, the bigger 2-liter bottles produce a better effect. The *Tornado Tube* is specially designed to screw onto the top of a standard plastic soda bottle.

You'll want to see what is going on inside the bottle, so it's important to remove the label and clean up the outside of the bottle. Here are some helpful hints:

- Rinse the bottle out using warm water.
- Remove the plastic ring that was once part of the screw-on cap from the top of the bottle. The plastic ring will prevent the *Tornado Tube* from being screwed onto the bottle all of the way and will cause the bottle to leak.
- Remove the label by completely filling the bottle with warm water, and let the bottle sit for 2 or 3 minutes. The warm water will melt the glue on the label making it easy to peel off the label.

Right Way!   Wrong Way!

The Inspiration Behind This Book

I can remember receiving my first *Tornado Tube* as a gift from a friend who is a science teacher. The words on the package said, "Create a tornado in a bottle!" How could a plastic tube help to make a tornado in a bottle? I must admit that I was a little skeptical, but I could not wait to get home to try it out.

My wife was cooking dinner when I walked through the front door with the *Tornado Tube* in my hand. I asked Renée for two empty plastic soda bottles in order to conduct an experiment, but unfortunately all of the bottles had been recycled the day before.

So I did what any impatient scientist would do under these circumstances. I ran to the store to buy two bottles of any soda that was cheap. Of course, all I really cared about were the plastic soda bottles and not what was inside them. In a matter of seconds, I was in the express check-out lane with two bottles of *Generic Pineapple-Banana-Grapefruit Soda*.

I'm sure that my wife thought I had lost my marbles when I came running through the front door with two bottles of generic soda in my hands making a mad dash for the kitchen sink. Since I only needed the bottles and not what was in them, I unscrewed the cap and started to pour the soda down the drain.

It didn't take long for me to figure out by the look in her eyes that Renée was not pleased with my wastefulness. Consequently, dinner that evening consisted of a lovely pasta dish, steamed broccoli, a dinner roll, and 4 liters of *Generic Pineapple-Banana-Grapefruit* soda. Fortunately, the extreme bloated feeling in my stomach subsided and I was happily making swirling tornadoes in my 2-liter bottles the rest of the night.

My fascination with the *Tornado Tube* didn't stop there. Over the course of the next few weeks, I introduced everyone I knew, and even people I didn't know, to my newly discovered science toy. The amazing thing is that when people played with the *Tornado Tube*, they would undoubtedly say, "What would happen if I did this...?" These seemingly innocent questions soon turned into experiments which were refined and ultimately found their way into this book.

Meet Craig Burnham,
The Inventor of the Tornado Tube

Have you ever thought about who
invents toys? What college do you go
to if you want to be a creator of toys?
Can you get a graduate degree in toy
making?

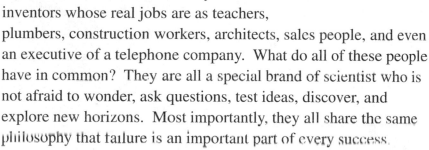

Over the past five years, I have had
the wonderful opportunity of meeting
a great number of successful toy
inventors whose real jobs are as teachers,
plumbers, construction workers, architects, sales people, and even
an executive of a telephone company. What do all of these people
have in common? They are all a special brand of scientist who is
not afraid to wonder, ask questions, test ideas, discover, and
explore new horizons. Most importantly, they all share the same
philosophy that failure is an important part of every success.

Many of the toys and products that these people invented were
discovered as the result of the failure of another experiment. Such is
the case with the inventor of the *Tornado Tube*, Craig Burnham. Craig
lives in Salem, Massachusetts, and owns a marine construction
company. How does someone who specializes in subaqueous
excavation of sand and rock come to invent a 2-liter soda bottle science
toy? Craig actually invented the *Tornado Tube* as a young boy in
1964, and Craig used profits from his construction company to secure
the patent and finance the development of the product some 25 years
later.

As a young boy, Craig was always tinkering with odds and ends found
around the house, trying to build whatever contraption came to mind.
He happened to be in his father's cellar one day when he got the idea
to build a large, homemade hourglass. Using two glass gallon-size

bottles, a piece of plastic irrigation tubing, a metal washer, and a couple of radiator hose clamps, Craig connected the two bottles in the shape of an hourglass. In between the mouths of the bottles he placed a washer to control the flow of the salt.

The first problem that he encountered was not in the design of the hourglass, but what went in it. The sand that he collected outside was wet and clogged the bottles. Table salt would probably work better than sand, but Craig couldn't find the amount of salt needed to fill the bottles. So, out of necessity, Craig made yet another substitution. He filled one of the bottles with plain water.

With the water in place and the hose and clamps secured, Craig was ready to test his theory. Unfortunately, when Craig turned his attention away from the workbench for just a split second, the top-heavy glass bottles fell over and broke on the floor.

Still determined to make it work, Craig built another water hourglass, but this time he used two quart-size bottles. He predicted that the water from the top bottle would flow down and fill the empty bottle just like sand would flow from the top of the hourglass to fill the bottom. He turned the bottles over putting the one full of water on top, and he watched as only a small amount of water dripped from the top bottle to the bottom bottle. Then, the water flow completely stopped. Why, he wondered? Craig repeated the experiment and again the water would not flow smoothly between the bottles.

His initial failure resulted in taking the bottles apart and changing the size of the metal washer that was between the mouths of the bottles. Maybe the hole in the washer was too small, and the water could not easily flow through the opening. Even with a larger washer, the water was getting stuck in the top bottle. As Craig explains it, "The silly thing just didn't work."

Craig could not understand why it didn't work even after a number of modifications. Finally, in a fit of frustration, he shook the bottles and exclaimed, "Why doesn't it work?"

Then something very unusual happened. Shaking the bottles caused the water in the middle of the top bottle to swirl in the shape of a tornado. Even though he was no longer shaking the bottle, the water continued to swirl, moving faster and faster from the upper bottle to the lower bottle. He stood in amazement staring at the bottles on the workbench.

Craig was afraid he couldn't do it again. *Maybe it was a one-time phenomenon*, he thought. Yet, whenever he swirled the bottles in a clockwise or counterclockwise direction, the tornado appeared, and mysteriously the water easily flowed from one bottle to the other.

Craig didn't really have any big plans for his *Tornado Tube* invention. He made a few for his friends, gave a few away as Christmas gifts, and then tucked his creation away for almost 25 years. In 1987, he revisited the idea with plans this time to turn it into a science toy using recycled 2-liter plastic soda bottles. The cost of obtaining a patent to protect his idea and developing a mold to manufacture the *Tornado Tube* was quite expensive. Craig thought to himself, *Would anyone want to buy this toy?*

After careful consideration, Craig completed the necessary paperwork for his patent and was awarded his patent one year later. He designed the mold for the tube, and in just a short time was in the science toy manufacturing business. Over time, the living room of his home was turned into a place to package the *Tornado Tube*, and everyone in his family pitched in to help fill the orders.

Little did Craig know that 25 years after experimenting in his father's cellar with glass bottles, hoses, and clamps, he would go on to manufacture one of the most popular and successful science toys in the world.

Chapter 2

It's a Vortex

It's a Vortex

The swirling tornado in the bottle is referred to as a *vortex*, which is a type of motion that causes liquids and gases to travel in spirals around a center line. When you pull the plug on the bathtub drain, the water spins in the form of a vortex. Gusty winds often produce miniature tornadoes called *dust devils*. A vortex will continue its rotating action naturally until something occurs to stop it.

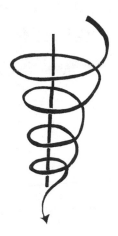

How Does a Vortex Start?

Vortices (that's the plural form of vortex) form in many ways. A vortex can be created when a rotating liquid falls through an opening. Gravity is the force that pulls the liquid into the hole and a continuous vortex develops. Only a small amount of swirling action is needed to start the vortex.

You can see a vortex form over the drain when you let the water out of a bathtub. You'll notice that the water spins away from the center of the vortex. The rotating motion of the water pushes it outward as it spirals into the drain. The vortex will continue until the water is gone, unless you cover the drain or block the rotation.

Did You Know?

Water running down a drain will rotate in a different direction in the Northern and Southern Hemispheres. If water runs out from a perfectly symmetrical bathtub, or toilet bowl, in the Northern Hemisphere it would swirl counterclockwise, and water would spin clockwise in the Southern Hemisphere. This phenomenon is due to the Coriolis effect, which is the influence that the Earth's rotation has on any moving body of water or air. This explains the counterclockwise or clockwise rotation of water as it flows down the drain.

The Coriolis Effect: Looking for Answers

In September of 1994, Ms. Brunner's sixth-grade science class at Holden Middle School in Holden, Missouri, decided to research the Coriolis effect on their own. The students wanted to know if the direction of the swirling water *really* does change depending on whether it is in the Northern or Southern Hemisphere. Indeed, the students could test the Northern Hemisphere theory right in their classroom, but taking the whole class on a field trip to South America would be impossible!

Ms. Brunner was not going to let a few thousand miles stand in her way. While she didn't have the resources to *physically* take the class to South America, she could take the students anywhere in the world by means of a computer and the Internet. She decided to use the Internet to post her students' question and hope that a scientist or group of scientists who specialized in fluid dynamics could supply some answers.

The question was posted on an information forum on the Internet at 5:50 pm, on September 6, 1994. Within two hours the first response came in from South America. In Columbia, the reply stated, "Water goes down the drain in the opposite direction that it does in your

Northern Hemisphere." Then, from an observer in Ecuador, very near the equator, Ms. Brunner's students learned that water goes straight down the drain. There was not much in the way of a scientific explanation, just observations made by other human beings in different parts of the world. This Information Superhighway exercise demonstrated to the students that they were actually contributing to the field of knowledge and experiencing first-hand the thrill of scientific exploration.

However, the story doesn't end here. During the next four days, scientists from all over the world replied to the students' questions. Comments and theories came from Arkansas, Indiana, Louisiana, Massachusetts, Missouri, New Jersey, and South Carolina. Replies also came from Argentina, Australia, Brazil, Columbia, and Ecuador. At the outset, the students probably never imagined calling a professor at MIT or Loyola University or a government agency for an answer to their seemingly simple question. Yet, scientists from all over the world responded to their scientific inquiries. Generally speaking, the scientists could not agree on any theory. Instead, they exchanged ideas and suggested ways for the students to test their hypothesis. Indeed, the students learned first-hand that theory guides and experiment decides. Ms. Brunner firmly believes that the students learned more about the true nature of science from their experience than any textbook could ever supply.

Finding a Vortex in Nature

A vortex can also form behind a blunt object sitting in a stream of flowing liquid or gas. For example, a vortex may form behind a rock in a creek. The flowing water splits into two streams as it hits the rock. When these two streams meet on the other side of the rock, they will be flowing toward each other. Some rotational action may occur and a vortex may form. This vortex is called a whirlpool.

You can think of the wind blowing (or flowing) around a building in the same way. When the two air streams meet behind the building, they may form a vortex. Have you ever seen the leaves on the side of your house blow around in a circle for a few seconds? That so-called dust-devil is a vortex.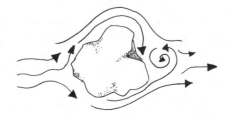

Vortices can form in water or air when two streams flow against each other. In the atmosphere, winds moving in two directions with different temperatures can affect the weather. They may form local vortices known as tornadoes or very large, regional vortices known as hurricanes.

Chapter 3

The Science
of the Tornado

Tornadoes and other Whirling Windstorms

Natural atmospheric processes produce amazingly powerful storms. Two types of storms result when winds and water combine in just the right way to produce violent vortices. These storms are tornadoes and hurricanes.

Both types of storms are associated with thunderstorms. A tornado occurs over land and is formed within a thunderstorm. A hurricane is formed by many thunderstorms over the ocean combined in a rotating pattern. Tornadoes are much smaller than hurricanes, but have much stronger winds. Hurricanes that pass over land can start tornadoes.

All About Tornadoes

A tornado is a fierce windstorm that becomes a powerful rotating column of air. The violent winds of a tornado are the strongest winds on earth. They form a high speed vortex rotating around a region of low atmospheric pressure and temperature in the tornado's center.

Winds in a tornado spiral upwards. The whirling power of these updrafts pulls dirt, trees, and other objects from the ground and into the storm.

Tornadoes are also called twisters or cyclones because of their swirling winds. A tornado that forms over water or leaves the land to travel over water becomes a waterspout.

Tornadoes have incredible power. These storms injure and kill people and destroy property. A tornado can drive a fork into a tree, lift a car into the air, or break the trunk of a thick tree as if it were a twig.

How Does a Tornado Start?

The word "tornado" comes from the Spanish word *tornada* which means "thunderstorm." Although a tornado is not a thunderstorm, it usually forms during a severe thunderstorm.

The conditions required to produce tornadoes occur often in the spring and summer in the Central and Midwestern United States. Dry, cold air travels south from Canada. Warm air drifts north from the Gulf of Mexico. This warm air contains moisture. A weather "front" occurs along the line where the cool air meets the warm, moist air. Fronts can extend for hundreds of miles.

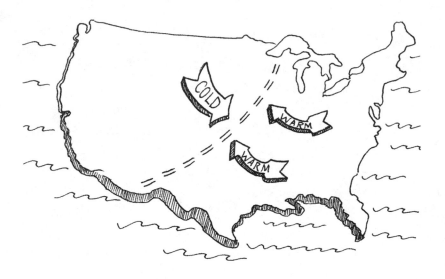

When the two kinds of air meet, the cold air tries to slip down and move along the ground. Warm air pushes upward and the moisture in the warm air condenses and forms water droplets as this air is cooled. These water droplets form clouds. All along the front, a line of large cumulonimbus clouds begins to grow. These giant, beautiful clouds are often called thunderclouds or thunderheads.

The ground is hot from the sun and the cold air begins to heat up and tries to rise. Columns of rising air are known as updrafts. Warm air becomes trapped near the ground, under the layer of incoming cold air. When the warm air finally breaks through, an updraft rises like a fountain up through the cold air and into the sky. That is why

thunderheads look so tall. They can grow to over 10 miles high. When the thunderhead becomes high enough to reach the jet stream, it can be affected by extremely powerful winds traveling eastward from the Pacific Ocean. Slower winds near the ground are also acting on the thunderhead. The rising air may start to spin and form a rotating updraft, which results in the making of a severe thunderstorm.

This rotating updraft is a vortex, and it usually forms near the mid-section of a thunderhead. As the rotation becomes stronger, the vortex gets longer and thinner. It may form a column that stretches down through the thunderhead. A column of spinning winds is called a mesocyclone. It is the next step on the way to the formation of a tornado.

A mesocyclone may spin for a while and then vanish. Sometimes, one begins to spin in tighter spirals near the ground. When this section dips down from the bottom of the mesocyclone, it is called a funnel cloud. A funnel cloud is the last step before the formation of a tornado. The funnel cloud becomes a tornado when it finally touches the ground.

Some funnel clouds are invisible, because the air near the ground has no moisture left. If no water droplets form, no clouds will appear. We cannot see the whirling winds without the formation of clouds.

Did You Know?

Wind speeds have been estimated at 115 miles per hour for weak tornadoes and 300 miles per hour or faster for violent tornadoes.

A tornado is visible to us because of the water droplets it contains and the dirt and objects that it picks up as it travels across the land. Not all tornadoes are shaped like funnels. Some are shaped like columns or pillars. Very large, violent tornadoes may be so wide that they look like a storm cloud moving along the ground. Some large tornadoes generate smaller satellite tornadoes that circle the parent windstorm.

Remember that tornadoes usually occur during severe thunderstorms, so there are high winds, heavy rains, and falling hail all around. When the tornado approaches, it often becomes calm in the immediate area, because no rain or hail falls in the updraft of the whirling vortex.

Some people have been near enough to tornadoes to hear them. They report that tornadoes make a hissing snakelike sound, a whistling noise, or that they sound like hundreds of speeding train engines.

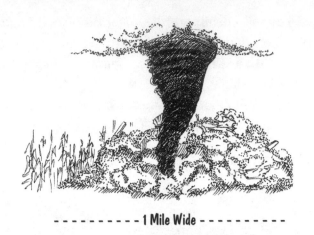

- - - - - - - - - - 1 Mile Wide - - - - - - - - - -

Dirt, trees, and other debris are lifted into the air by the swirling vortex. The path of destruction cut by a tornado is usually only as wide as the tornado. This means that a tornado can destroy one house and leave the house next door undisturbed. It can mow down the trees on one side of the road and leave those on the other side just as they were.

Some tornadoes have been as wide as one mile. Most are between 100 and 600 yards across. It may help you to picture their size if you remember that 100 yards is the length of a football field.

Tornadoes usually travel along the ground at 25 to 40 miles per hour. Some may travel at land speeds of 60 to 70 miles per hour.

Some tornadoes stay on the ground and continue to travel along until they lose their energy. Tornadoes can travel in straight lines or follow a winding path. Some lift into the air and drop back down somewhere else. They can last from a few seconds to a few hours.

The average tornado path is about 4 miles long, although some tornadoes travel along the ground for a hundred miles or more.

Between 600 and 900 tornadoes touch down in the United States in a typical year. The USA has more of these windstorms than any other country.

A dust devil is another kind of swirling windstorm. Dust devils are usually only a few feet wide and have wind speeds of under 30 miles per hour. A desert area is the most likely place to see a dust devil. They are formed when hot air starts to rise and spin near the ground. Dust devils are not usually associated with thunderstorms and can form under clear skies. They last from a few seconds to a few minutes.

Scientists have developed special radar equipment which helps them watch storms as they form. They have learned to recognize conditions that are likely to produce tornadoes. When the scientists at the National Weather Service see these conditions, they broadcast warnings for people in the area to find shelter.

You should pay close attention to tornado weather bulletins. They have helped to save many people from being hurt or killed in tornadoes. The Weather Service has been providing tornado warnings since 1953. Tornadoes used to kill about 230 people in the United States each year, because the people were unprepared. Warnings have lowered that number to about 120 people per year.

Chapter 4

All About Hurricanes

All About Hurricanes

Hurricanes are large, swirling wind and rain storms that may be hundreds of miles wide. Many large thunderstorms come together over ocean water and begin to swirl like a vortex. When this vortex becomes powerful enough, it is called a hurricane.

The fiercest winds of a hurricane occur near its center, in the "eye wall." This is the most damaging part of the storm. A cloud-free low pressure area forms in the center of the whirling vortex. This is the "eye" of the hurricane.

Hurricanes have enormous amounts of energy. One of these storms produces enough energy in one day to provide all the power consumed by some industrialized nations for an entire year. Hurricanes can uproot trees, demolish buildings, and cause flooding.

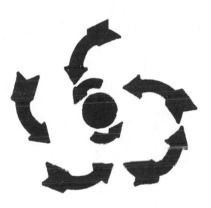

How Does a Hurricane Start?

The hurricane takes its name from the West Indian word *huracan* which means "big wind." Storms that occur over the Atlantic or the eastern Pacific Oceans are called hurricanes. The same kind of storm that forms over the western Pacific or Indian Oceans is called a typhoon. This name comes from the Chinese word *taifun* or "great wind." Hurricanes and typhoons are not just violent winds. They are giant, whirling storms that develop in a special way.

Hurricanes form only in the tropics where extremely moist air and heat are concentrated over the ocean, near the equator. The water temperature must be at least 80 degrees Fahrenheit both day and night.

A wet season with increased rainfall begins in late spring and lasts to early autumn. This is the time of year when hurricanes develop.

Evaporation of the warm water into the atmosphere over the ocean makes the air very moist. Winds blowing across the ocean in different directions begin to push masses of warm, moist air toward each other. This event is called convergence.

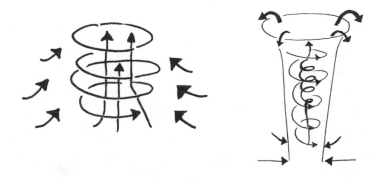

When the air masses collide, the air in the center starts to rise, forming an updraft. At high altitudes, the moist air of the updraft begins to cool and water droplets form. These water droplets form clouds.

Large cumulonimbus clouds begin to grow and thunderstorms develop. More thunderstorms form as more convergence and updrafts occur. If the thunderstorms do not dissipate, they may start to gather together. This formation is called a tropical disturbance.

Many more thunderstorms join the disturbance. This weather event becomes large enough to be influenced by forces created from the earth's rotation. The tropical disturbance begins to swirl and becomes a vortex of thunderstorms.

Updrafts are continuously pulling more air into the disturbance. When the winds begin to blow continuously at 23 miles per hour, the storm becomes a tropical depression. The tropical depression continues to

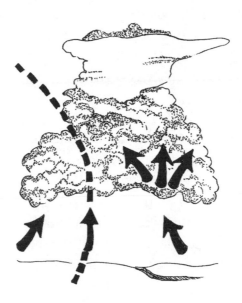

gain power and becomes a tropical storm when the wind speed becomes 40 miles per hour.

At any time, the disturbance, depression, or storm can run out of hot, moist air and weaken or die out. If it continues to gain strength and reaches 74 miles per hour, it is called a hurricane.

Did You Know?

Hurricanes have top wind speeds of at least 74 miles per hour, but wind speed can reach 180 miles per hour. The closer you are to the storm's center, the faster the wind will be. The top wind speed will be reached within 60 miles from the center of the hurricane. As you move away from the center, wind speed is slower. At 300 miles from the center, the wind speed may be only 18 miles per hour.

The energy of a hurricane comes from the heat released when water vapor condenses to liquid water. The atmosphere above a tropical ocean is the only place enough warm, moist air is available to produce the energy necessary to create a hurricane.

If you could view a hurricane from a space shuttle orbit, you would see a large circular pattern of beautiful white clouds swirling over the blue ocean. These storms are so large that this is the only way you could see the whole hurricane at once.

When you are on the Earth in the path of a hurricane, you will see it from inside. Very few people have survived being inside a tornado, but millions of people have survived being inside a hurricane.

Imagine you are on a tropical island and a hurricane passes over you. You will feel the wind begin to get stronger as the sky darkens. The weather gets worse and there are strong winds, lightning, heavy rain, and hail all around you. When the eye of the hurricane passes over you, the fiercest winds die down. The sky will lighten and you may think the storm is over. Watch out! When the eye has passed, the storm will be back. The winds will be blowing in the opposite direction now because they are really blowing in a giant circle. You are on the other side of the circle this time.

The movement of a hurricane is somewhat predictable. It is so large that it moves with the earth's wind currents that surround it. These wind currents are very large and steady and do not change course abruptly; therefore, hurricanes usually travel in one of these wind currents until they meet another wind current, then they may change direction. If a hurricane changes course, it could pass over the same area twice. Sometimes one of these storms stalls over an area for days.

A hurricane covers a very large area. Sometimes a tropical storm can have a cloud system that is 2,000 miles in diameter. Typically, a hurricane is about 300 miles across. That is about the distance from Chicago, Illinois to Columbus, Ohio. An average hurricane is about 800 to 5,000 times as wide as an average tornado.

Hurricanes usually travel across the sea and land at 10 to 32 miles per hour. Some may travel at speeds up to 50 miles per hour. The path of a hurricane usually covers thousands of miles, most of it over the ocean.

Hurricanes last from several days to a week. They usually end when they reach cooler waters or pass over a large land mass. Sometimes, a hurricane will move across a peninsula or large island to another warm tropical water source and it will regain its strength. The hardest hit populated regions of any land mass are usually the coastal areas. When a hurricane passes over a large land mass, the severe thunderstorms within it may produce tornadoes.

Although the strong winds of a hurricane can cause considerable damage to property, water damage is usually the most costly problem. The moisture released as rainfall in a typical hurricane can be ten inches in one day. The largest storms can result in up to 24 inches of rain in that period. In addition, the strong winds produce unusually high waves and tides that often flood coastal cities, towns and settlements.

Hurricanes are common weather patterns that are a very natural part of the earth's seasonal cycles. Usually, the Atlantic Ocean experiences about five hurricanes each year. These and less intense tropical storms bring needed rain to coastal regions.

Scientists use pictures taken from satellites to observe tropical storms and to spot hurricanes as they develop. Before satellite pictures were available, people had to rely on reports from weather stations and ships. Since hurricanes form at sea, many were not observed in time for effective warning.

It is very important to track these huge storms and to make accurate predications about their movements. Many people live in areas affected by hurricanes. If the National Hurricane Center scientists believe a hurricane is threatening to reach a populated area within 24 hours, they will issue a hurricane warning. People prepare by gathering and sheltering property and boarding up homes and businesses. Sometimes people will even be evacuated from an area if the forecast calls for an extremely strong storm. Many lives have been saved by these preparations.

To study conditions inside hurricanes, teams of pilots and weather scientists fly regular missions into these storms. They get measurements of wind speed, temperature, air pressure, and other weather conditions at different altitudes. These investigations help scientists make predictions about hurricane formation and movement.

The National Weather Service names hurricanes to quickly identify them. The names are assigned in alphabetical order alternating between female and male names. There are separate lists of names for hurricanes in the Atlantic and Pacific oceans.

Chapter 5

Hands-on Activities and Experiments with the Tornado Tube

A Word About These Experiments

By now, you know what the *Tornado Tube* does, who invented it, the science of the vortex, and all about tornadoes and hurricanes, but there's more!

During the summer of 1995, the idea of organizing a *Tornado Tube* Creativity Contest was born at the *Hands-on Science Institute* at Regis University in Denver, Colorado. The staff gave every teacher and student in the summer science program their very own *Tornado Tube*. Their personal challenge was to come up with something unusual, practical, creative, or nonsensical to do with an ordinary *Tornado Tube*. Up until this point, most people were content with the notion that the *Tornado Tube* simply created a swirling vortex of water in a soda bottle. We wanted to push the limits and challenge our summer scientists to use their creative genius...and they did!

Nearly 300 students and teachers worked together to develop an incredible collection of hands-on activities and scientific discoveries.

Students and teachers who are credited with the following ideas are from Colorado and the schools mentioned are located in Colorado unless otherwise noted.

The Original Tornado Tube Experiment

Use the *Tornado Tube* to connect two plastic soda bottles, one of which is partially filled with water. By simply rotating the bottles in a circular motion, the water inside swirls in the shape of a vortex creating the appearance of a tornado. Craig Burnham from Salem, Massachusetts, invented the *Tornado Tube* in 1964 and made it available for sale in 1987.

Procedure

1. You will need two empty 2-liter clear plastic soda bottles. Fill one bottle 2/3 full with water and attach the *Tornado Tube*.
2. Attach the second bottle to the other end of the *Tornado Tube*. Make sure that the bottles are screwed on securely so that the water does not leak.
3. Place the connected bottles on a flat surface with the empty bottle on the bottom. What happens? Why doesn't the water begin to flow down from the top bottle?

Here's why: Even though the bottom bottle appears empty, it is really filled with air. Since air occupies the space in the lower bottle, the water cannot flow into the bottom bottle unless the air has somewhere to go.

4. Hold the end of the top bottle and swirl it in a circular motion until a vortex develops. The circular motion of the bottles causes the water to rotate in a circular motion. The force of gravity is acting on the water in the upper bottle and the water is dropping through the hole in the *Tornado Tube*. Notice that the water avoids the center of the vortex and the air from the bottom bottle is able to flow upward through the vortex into the top bottle.

The Quick-Pour Soda Bottle Race

How long does it take to empty a 2-liter soda bottle full of water? You'll amaze your friends and explore some of the scientific properties of air and water when you try this quick-pour method.

Procedure

You'll need an empty 2-liter soda bottle and a large pitcher of water or access to a sink and a stopwatch or watch with a second hand to record your times.

1. Fill the soda bottle to the top with water. If you do not have access to a sink nearby, use a large pitcher to fill the bottle.
2. How long will it take to empty all of the water in the bottle into the pitcher on the table? Record your prediction on a piece of paper.
3. Without squeezing the sides of the bottle or swirling the liquid, time how long it takes to empty all of the water. Repeat this 3 times and write down how long it takes on your piece of paper. Your data table might look something like this:

Method	Time #1	Time #2	Time #3
Glug-Glug			

Try the Quick-Pour Method

Can you think of a way to empty the water faster without squeezing the sides of the bottle? Here's a hint: create a vortex in the bottle. Fill the bottle to the top with water just as you did before. However, this time give the bottle a clockwise or counterclockwise swirl. Notice what happens. The water begins to swirl in the shape of a vortex and flows out of the bottle very quickly. Why?

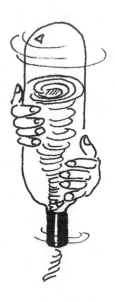

Time how long it takes to empty the soda bottle using the vortex method. Record your times below.

Method	Time #1	Time #2	Time #3
Swirl			

Explanation

The action of swirling the water in the bottle while you are pouring it out causes the formation of a vortex. The vortex looks like a tornado in the bottle. The opening of the vortex allows air molecules to rush into the bottle, while at the same time the water flows out of the bottle. If you do not swirl the water and just allow it to flow out on its own, then the air and water have to essentially take turns passing through the mouth of the bottle.

You might want to demonstrate the *Quick-Pour Soda Bottle Race* before showing someone your *Tornado Tube*.

Tornado Tube Racer

Let's use the *Tornado Tube* in a different way and see how far we can roll two connected bottles. Each time, we'll add more water to the bottles. Will the bottles roll a longer or shorter distance as we add water?

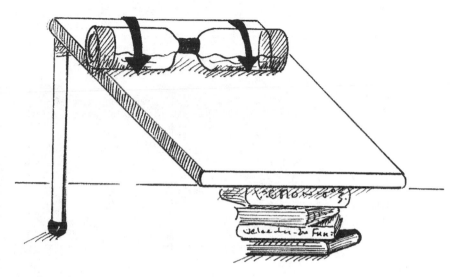

Pre-Race Preparation

- For each race, you'll need to measure the same amount of water into each bottle and then connect the bottles. Some people find it easy to use a funnel and a measuring cup, or you might want to use a specially made measuring bowl, the kind with a pouring spout.

- Make a copy of the sample data table on the following page. It will be important to keep track of the results of each race so that you can analyze the information later.

- Make sure that you have a tape measure handy to record the distance the bottles traveled at the end of each race.

- The race starts with the bottles resting at the top of a ramp. You might want to use a large piece of cardboard or a thin sheet of wood for your ramp. Raise one side with a block of wood or a pile of books to make a ramp. Put a piece of masking tape across the top of the ramp. This will be your starting line.

DATA TABLE

Race	Amount of Water in Bottle	Distance Traveled Measure to the Connector
#1	Empty	_____
#2	1/4 Full	_____
#3	1/2 Full	_____
#4	3/4 Full	_____
#5	Completely Full	_____

Race #1

1. The first race will be run with empty soda bottles. Connect the two bottles with the *Tornado Tube*.
2. Lay the connected bottles on their sides and hold them just behind the starting line. Release them and let the bottles roll down the ramp until they stop.
3. Use the tape measure to measure from the starting line to the location of the *Tornado Tube* connector. Record this distance on your data table.

Race #2

1. Fill each bottle 1/4 full with water. Measure carefully so that the bottles have the same amount of water in each.
2. Lay the connected bottles on their sides and hold them just behind the starting line. Release them and let the bottles roll down the ramp until they stop. Watch the bottles closely. Where does the water go as the bottles roll? Does it whirl around in the bottles or stay at the lowest point of each bottle?
3. Use the tape measure to measure from the starting line to the location of the *Tornado Tube* connector. Record this distance on your data table.

Races #3, 4, 5

1. Fill each bottle 1/2 full with water. Measure carefully so that the bottles have the same amount of water in each.
2. Lay the connected bottles on their sides and hold them just behind the starting line. Release them and let the bottles roll down the ramp until they stop.
3. Use the tape measure to measure from the starting line to the location of the *Tornado Tube* connector. Record this distance on your data table.
4. Repeat steps 1 through 3, but this time fill the bottles 3/4 full for Race #4 and fill the bottles completely full for Race #5. Remember to measure accurately and record your results on the data table.

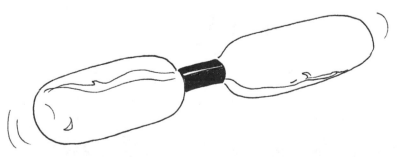

Examine Your Results

Look closely at the distances that you recorded on the data table. As you added more water, did the rolling distance get longer or shorter? How did this compare with your prediction?

Explanation

Gravity acts on the bottles as they roll down the ramp. The more mass that is present, the stronger the force that is exerted on the bottles. Since more force is "pulling" the bottles when they contain water, we are inclined to think that the bottles will roll farther.

You probably also found that the bottles rolled the longest distance when they were *empty*. That is because inertia is acting on the water in the bottles. This means that the water does not rotate along with the bottles. It is resisting the motion of the bottles and slowing them down. You saw this happening if you watched the bottles closely. Did you notice that the water always stayed at the lowest point in the bottles? Gravity and inertia were keeping the water there. Remember that friction also acts on the bottles and slows them down. Your bottles will roll farther on a smooth floor than on a carpeted one.

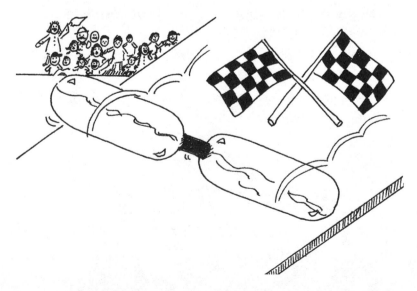

Tornado Tube Race Follow-up Ideas

Scientists usually repeat experiments many times. If results are different, they want to find out what caused the change. You may want to repeat your experiment in exactly the same way two more times. Do you get the same measurements in each test?

What are some reasons that you may get different measurements when you repeat this experiment? Do the different measurements change your conclusions?

Other variables in this experiment are the height and length of the ramp. Try raising or lowering your ramp to see how this change affects your results. You may want to find a wide board or another table that is longer or shorter than your original ramp. Repeat your tests and see how the results change.

Try repeating your tests with all the water in one of the bottles instead of divided between the two. What happens?

How Fast Does It Flow?

As you read earlier, Craig Burnham invented the *Tornado Tube* as a child when he was trying to make an inexpensive hour glass. He substituted water in place of salt and discovered some amazing results, namely the formation of a vortex.

In this experiment, you will figure out the relationship between the amount of water in the bottle and how fast it flows from one bottle to the other. If you think that you already know the answer, you might be surprised by what you find.

Experiment #1

1. Fill one of the bottles 3/4 full with water.
2. Connect the two bottles using the *Tornado Tube*.
3. Turn the bottles upside down but <u>do</u> <u>not</u> swirl the water. Let the bottles rest upright on the table and observe what happens to the water.

Explanation

When you turn the bottles upside down so that the bottle that is full of water is on top, some of the water spills down into the bottom bottle but stops flowing after a few seconds. Why? The bottom bottle is filled with air and air occupies space. In order for the water to flow into the bottom bottle, the air that occupies space in the lower bottle has to move to the upper bottle. Remember, even though you cannot see the air, it does take up space in the bottle. When you swirl the water in the bottle and form a vortex, the air from the lower bottle passes through the vortex while the water falls down into the bottom bottle.

Experiment #2

1. For this experiment you will need a measuring pitcher (a measuring cup will work but will take longer). Fill one of the 2-liter bottles with 8 ounces of water (approximately 1 cup or 250 milliliters).
2. Connect the other bottle using the *Tornado Tube*.
3. Use a partner to help you with this next step. One person should turn the connected bottles upside down, swirl them and set them on a flat surface with the empty bottle on the bottom. The job of the other person is to use a stopwatch or the second hand on a clock to time how long it takes for the water to flow from the top bottle to the empty bottle on the bottom.
4. You and your partner may want to practice this step several times to make sure that you can each do your job in the same way every time. If a vortex does not form when you swirl the water, try again with more swirling action.
5. The person with the stopwatch should stop the time when the last of the water flows into the bottom bottle. On your chart, record the time it took to empty the bottle.
6. Repeat the experiment several times using different amounts of water. For instance, try using 16 ounces of water instead of 8 ounces.

Complete the Data Table

Complete the data table on the following page by recording the amount of time in seconds that it takes to empty the bottle. Several trials are recommended so that you can average the times to get a more accurate reading.

DATA TABLE

Test	Amount of Water in the Bottle	Time to Empty the Water in the Bottle	Calculate the FLOW RATE
#1	8 ounces	_____	_____
#2	16 ounces	_____	_____
#3	24 ounces	_____	_____
#4	32 ounces	_____	_____
#5	40 ounces	_____	_____

Calculating the Flow Rate

Two cups of water is equal to 16 volume ounces of water. On the metric side, 2 cups of water is equal to approximately 500 milliliters. Let's use ounces for our example and then you can repeat the calculation using milliliters later. We want to find out how many ounces of water flow through the *Tornado Tube* per second. Here's what we have to do:

✓ Divide the number of ounces of water (16 ounces) by the time that it took the water to flow from the top bottle to the bottom bottle. For example, if you started with 16 ounces of water and it took 10 seconds to completely empty from the top to the bottom, then the flow rate is 16 ounces divided by 10 seconds = 1.6 ounces per second.

✓ The number you calculate is called the FLOW RATE and tells you how fast the water was flowing. In other words, how many ounces of water went from one bottle to the other in one second?

✓ Calculate the flow rate for the different amounts of water and compare your results. As you added more water, did the water flow faster or slower? How did this compare to your prediction?

Explanation

As you add more water, both the volume and the mass of the water in the bottles increase. It's only logical to conclude that it will take longer for the water to move from one bottle to the other as you increase the volume. However, your data from the experiment shows you that as the amount of water increases so does the flow rate or the speed of the water passing through the *Tornado Tube*.

Remember that the force of gravity is acting on the water to pull it through the hole in the *Tornado Tube*. The greater the mass of water in the bottle, the stronger the force that is exerted on the water by gravity. This actually makes the water flow faster through the *Tornado Tube*.

When scientists do experiments they usually repeat them many times to verify their results. If results are different, scientists want to find out what caused them to change. You may want to repeat your experiment two more times. Do you get the same time measurements in each test? What are some reasons that you may get different time measurements when you repeat this experiment?

Follow-up Idea

Do all liquids have the same flow rate? Conduct the flow rate experiment on other types of liquids like milk, vegetable oil, salt water, soda, tea, or any other liquid of your choice (and your parent's choice!). Record your observations on a new data table and explain your results. This might be a great science fair project.

Dorothy's Spinning House

How is the vortex in the *Tornado Tube* similar to a naturally occurring tornado, and in what important ways is it different?

Procedure

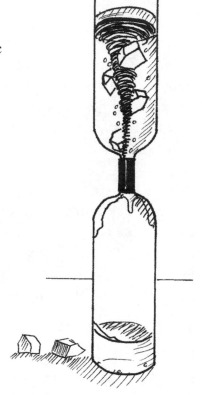

1. You'll need to find an assortment of miniature plastic houses, barnyard animals, beads, glitter, and whatever else you can find to recreate Dorothy's famous tornado in the *Wizard of Oz*.

2. Place the houses in the bottle and fill it 2/3 full with water. Attach the *Tornado Tube* and the second soda bottle.

3. Swirl the water in the bottle until a vortex appears. Notice what happens to the houses.

4. Repeat the swirling motion several times. Observe the vortex closely and answer these questions:

- Where are the plastic houses located before swirling the water, and where do they move to once the vortex forms?
- Do the houses move in a similar pattern each time?
- What did you observe about the *Tornado Tube* vortex that is similar to a naturally occurring tornado?
- What differences did you discover?

Explanation

In both cases, the vortex motion causes liquids or gases to travel in spirals around a core. As the water swirls, it pulls the houses and the other debris around with it. These items are not connected so each piece moves according to the speed of the water at different parts of the vortex.

The vortex action in the bottle is created by rotating water (a liquid), while air (a gas) is rotating in a natural tornado. Another difference is the direction of the vortex. The vortex in the bottle spirals downward. The winds in a tornado spiral upward.

Thank you to Lauren Mann from Kendrick Lake Elementary and Dennis Buchholz from Centennial Elementary for contributing their ideas for this activity.

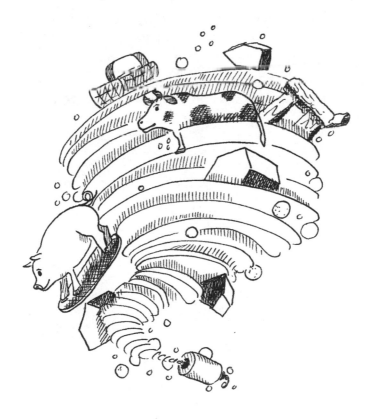

Science at the Movies

It seems that everyone got caught up in the science of tornadoes during the spring of 1996 with the release of the motion picture *Twister*. Hollywood sensationalized the practice of tornado-chasing scientists and the drama of surviving the fury of a raging F5 twister.

Shortly after the first printing of this book, United Artists Theaters in Denver asked us to set-up a display of *Tornado Tube* inventions for the opening of the movie. Movie-goers of all ages were seen swirling liquids in bottles and pondering the true force of nature's own tornadoes. Ok, some people just enjoyed the pretty colors!

The movie also inspired a number of *Tornado Tube* enthusiasts who wanted to test out a small-scale version of the special effects seen in the movie. Of course, there were a select few who couldn't wait to get home to fill their bottles with plastic houses and a few minature cows. Others, however, considered recreating the movement of the mirrored ball-like transmitters in the twisting vortex. Are these objects really drawn into the eye of the tornado or do they behave differently? Test it out with a few odds and ends from your local craft store. You might be surprised.

Mixing Colors

If you mix red and yellow water, what color will you see? In this activity, you'll use the swirling action of the vortex to mix color in a most unique way.

Procedure

1. Fill each bottle 1/3 full with water. Put the bottles side by side to see that they contain even amounts of water.
2. Add 5 drops of red food coloring to one bottle and 5 drops of yellow food coloring to the other bottle.
3. Make a prediction. What color will the water be when the two colors are mixed?
4. Here's the tricky step that must be done over the sink! Attach the *Tornado Tube* to the top of one bottle and quickly turn the other bottle upside down and attach it to the *Tornado Tube*. The real challenge is to come up with a way to connect the two bottles without spilling any liquid.
5. Swirl the water to create a vortex.
6. What color did you predict the water would be? What color is it?
7. Repeat this experiment with red and blue food coloring and with yellow and blue food coloring. How well did you predict the results?

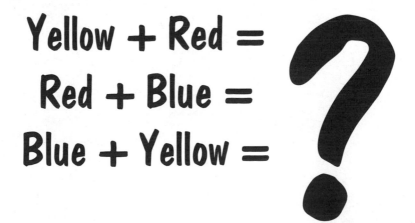

Yellow + Red =

Red + Blue =

Blue + Yellow =

Explanation

If you have measured the food coloring carefully, you should get orange when you mix red and yellow, violet when you mix red and blue, and green when you mix yellow and blue.

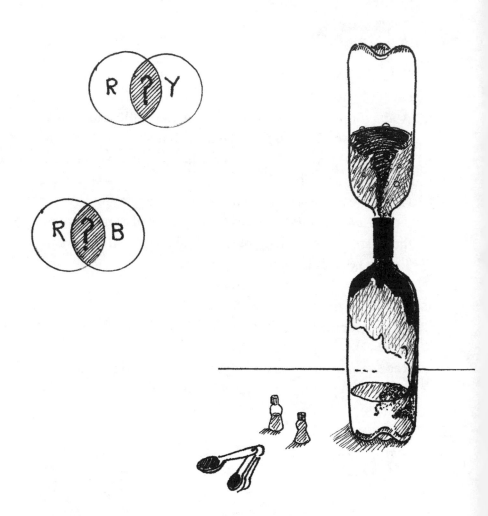

Vegetable Oil & Water Combo

Will oil and water mix together in a vortex? Some very unusual things happen when you try to make a slippery tornado.

> ASK PERMISSION: This activity requires the use of vegetable oil and food coloring. Be sure to ask permission before using these materials and be careful not to spill these liquids on the carpet or the furniture.

Procedure

1. Fill one of the plastic soda bottles half full with water.
2. Add 1 or 2 drops of food coloring.
3. Add approximately 1 cup of vegetable oil.
4. Connect the second bottle using the *Tornado Tube*. Make sure that the bottles are screwed together tightly so that the liquids do not leak.
5. Notice that the food coloring dyes the water but not the vegetable oil. Why?
6. Try to swirl the liquids in the bottle to create a vortex. How is this vortex different from the vortex that appears when you are using just plain water?

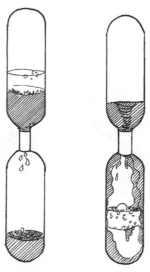

Explanation

#1: Oil and Water Don't Mix! The first thing that you probably notice is that the oil and water do not mix. In fact the oil floats on the surface of the water. Vegetable oil is an organic chemical compound that is *immiscible* with water. In other words, the oil will not stay mixed or blended with water, so they stay in separate layers.

#2: The Food Coloring Dilemma. Liquids that dissolve in each other are called *miscible*. The molecules of food coloring easily mix with the water molecules because food coloring is soluble or miscible in water.

#3: It Doesn't Work! Why is it difficult to make the vortex with oil and water? All fluids have a property known as *viscosity*. This is the measurable thickness or resistance to flow in a fluid. Honey and ketchup are liquids with a high resistance to flow. The viscosity of vegetable oil is not as high as that of honey, but it is considerably higher than that of water. When you swirl the oil and water in the bottle to make the vortex, the oil and water molecules do not move at the same rate because of their differences in viscosity. This results in the collapse of the vortex.

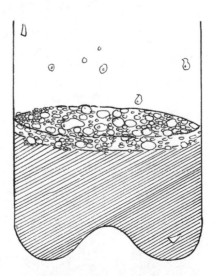

Twist of Color - *The Lamp Oil Solution*

Wouldn't it be amazing if you could color just the swirling vortex? Our first attempt with vegetable oil failed because of the differing thicknesses of the liquids. Believe it or not, we stumbled onto this swirling sensation by shear accident, and it's featured on the cover of this book. Check it out!

> WARNING: This experiment requires adult supervision. Use extreme caution when working with lamp oil. If you get any lamp oil on your skin, you should wash it off with soap and water immediately. Follow all safety instructions on the label of the lamp oil.

Procedure

1. You can purchase lamp oil at a local store where oil lanterns are sold. It's usually available in a variety of colors. For purposes of this experiment, let's assume that you are using red lamp oil.

2. Fill one of the plastic soda bottles 3/4 full with water.

3. Add approximately 1/4 cup of red lamp oil. Notice that the lamp oil does not mix with the water. Secondly, notice that the lamp oil has about the same thickness or viscosity as the water.

4. Attach the second bottle using the *Tornado Tube* connector. Make sure that the bottles are screwed together tightly so that the liquids do not leak.
5. Notice that the liquids are separated into two layers. Why?
6. Turn the bottles so that the liquids are on top and give the bottles a swirl. Don't take you eyes off the vortex!

As you are swirling the liquids, think about these questions:

- How is this vortex different than the vortex that appears when you just use water?
- How is this different from using vegetable oil?
- Are the liquids mixed when they reach the bottom bottle?

7. Try swirling the lamp oil and water mixture in the bottom bottle only. If you're using a smooth bottom bottle, you can create a colored vortex without even using the *Tornado Tube*.

Explanation

Remember, the goal of the activity was to color just the vortex in the bottle, and the lamp oil does the trick. Notice that the lamp oil has about the same viscosity or thickness as the water. Unlike the *Vegetable Oil and Water Combo* experiment, the lamp oil does not stop the flow of the vortex. Instead, the molecules of water and lamp oil spin at the same rate, and the less dense lamp oil is drawn toward the center of the vortex. Wow!

Suspended Colors

From your experimentation during the last activity, you know that oil and water do not mix. What happens when you add a few drops of food coloring to a bottle filled with just vegetable oil? It's guaranteed to get lots of "oohs" and "ahhs!"

Procedure

1. This activity uses vegetable oil in place of water. For this reason, you'll probably want to find the smallest bottles possible.
2. Fill one of the plastic soda bottles 1/2 full with vegetable oil.
3. Add a few drops of red, blue, green, and yellow food coloring to the vegetable oil. Notice that the food coloring and the oil do not mix. Why?
4. Attach the second bottle using the *Tornado Tube* connector.
4. <u>Try</u> to make a vortex by swirling the vegetable oil in the bottles. What happens to the suspended drops of color? Can you create a vortex? If not, how come?
5. What would happen if water was added to the mixture? Remember, food coloring mixes with water and not oil. What do you predict will happen to the tiny droplets of food coloring?

Explanation

Notice that the tiny drops of food coloring are suspended in the vegetable oil. Even when you swirl the oil and try to create a vortex, the oil and food coloring do not mix. Unfortunately, the vegetable oil is too thick to make a vortex. Try as you might, but the vortex never appears.

You might be inclined to think that the food coloring would color the oil, but the drops of color do not mix with the vegetable oil because food coloring is water-based. This means that it mixes with water but does not mix with oil. Oil and water are said to be immiscible, which means they do not mix but rather separate into layers.

If water is added to the mixture, the food coloring will eventually mix with the water. In doing so, the tiny drops burst into streams of color that fall to the bottom of the bottle and color the water black. It's a colorful finale to your twisting tornado.

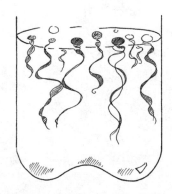

Tornado Tube Salad Dressing

Bring a science lesson to the dinner table as you use the vortex action to mix-up your favorite salad dressing.

Procedure

If you plan to eat your salad dressing, be sure to carefully wash the bottles and the *Tornado Tube* connector before starting. Unless you are planning to eat mass quantities of salad, you might want to find 1-liter soda bottles or smaller. Everyone has a favorite vinegar and oil dressing with their own special blend of spices. Substitute your favorite ingredients for those listed below.

1. Measure 1/2 cup of vinegar into a clean soda bottle.
2. Add 1 1/2 cups of vegetable oil.
3. Mix in 1 1/2 teaspoons of salt and 1/4 teaspoon of pepper or whatever seasonings you desire.

4. Attach the other clean bottle by means of the *Tornado Tube* connector.
5. Turn the bottles so that your salad dressing is on top and start the tornado action.
6. Describe what happens. Is the dressing mixed when it passes through the tube? Is it mixed when it reaches the bottom bottle? Does all the dressing go through the tube?
7. If necessary, continue to swirl the bottle until all the dressing flows through the tube. Does your salad dressing stay mixed? Remix your dressing as many times as you wish.
8. As soon as all of the dressing empties into the bottom bottle, unscrew the bottom bottle and pour the dressing over the top of the salad.

It's one thing to talk about science at the dinner table, but it's truly great to perform an experiment and then eat it. If you have questions as to why the liquids separated or why the vortex stopped swirling halfway through the experiment, refer to an earlier experiment called *Vegetable Oil & Water Combo*, on page 65, for a complete explanation.

Honey Mustard

6 oz. Rice wine vinegar
6 tsp. Honey
6 tsp. Hot Chinese mustard
3 tsp. Vegetable oil
Pinch of salt and pepper

Italian Herb

6 oz. Balsamic Vinegar
3 Tbsp. Olive oil
3 tsp. Dried basil
3 tsp. Ground oregano
3 tsp. Ground thyme
Dash of salt and pepper

French Vinaigrette

2 oz. Olive oil
4 oz. Red wine vinegar
2 Tbsp. Mixed parsley
2 tsp. Dijon mustard
1 tsp. Minced garlic
1 tsp. Sugar
Pinch of salt and pepper

Twister Tea

Jason Shin from Colorow Elementary quenches his thirst with a little *Twister Tea*.

Procedure

If you intend to drink your *Twister Tea*, be sure to carefully wash the bottles and the *Tornado Tube* connector before starting. Use 1 or 2-liter bottles depending on how much tea you want to make.

1. Fill one of the bottles 3/4 full with water.
2. Poke 2 or 3 tea bags down inside the plastic soda bottle being careful not to accidentally tear the bags. The number of tea bags that you use depends on how strong you like your tea. Adjust the length of the string on the bags so that the tea is touching the water.

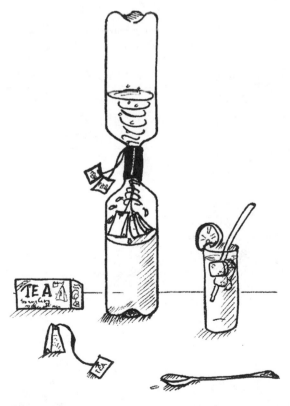

3. Hang the end of the strings over the neck of the bottle and use the *Tornado Tube* to hold the bags in place as shown in the illustration.

4. Attach the second bottle to the other end of the *Tornado Tube*.

5. Swirl the water in the bottles to form the vortex. As the water moves from one bottle to the other, it mixes with the tea. When you are finished swirling, allow the bottles to sit in the sun for a few hours to finish brewing.

Be the first on your block to enjoy an ice cold glass of *Twister Tea*.

Glitter Twister

Sprinkle a little of your favorite colored glitter in the water to make a vortex that is bespangled by twinkling sparkles. Don't limit your creativity to glitter alone. You will find a large variety of brightly colored confetti and mylar sprinkles at your local craft or hobby store.

Add a Little Lamp Oil..

Try adding approximately 1/4 cup of clear, colorless lamp oil to your glitter mixture. Since the lamp oil is less dense than the water, it floats to the top. When you swirl the liquids to make a vortex, the lamp oil is drawn to the middle of the vortex along with the glitter! Make one *Tornado Tube* set-up with lamp oil and another without lamp oil and compare the results.

The Tubular Pencil Holder

Brad White from Dennison Elementary found that his *Tornado Tube* made a perfect pencil holder on his desk. Simply insert the pencil or pen into the hole in the *Tornado Tube* and there you have it...a *Tornado Tube* Pencil Holder.

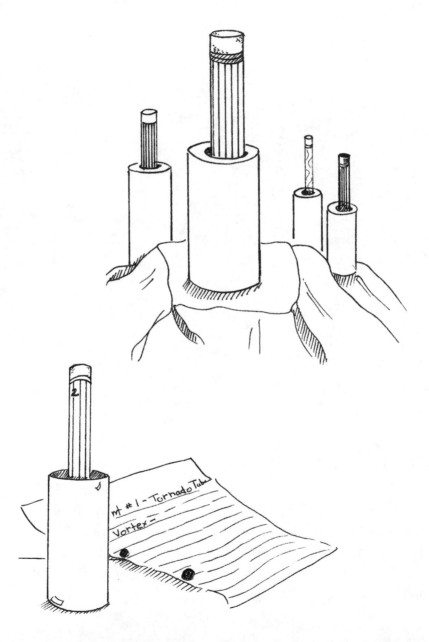

Vegetable Washer

Chris Wegman from Willow Creek Elementary found a practical use for his *Tornado Tube* in the kitchen. He invented the world's first vortex powered vegetable washer.

Procedure

1. Place several stalks of celery or carrot sticks in each of the two bottles.
2. Fill one of the bottles 1/2 full with water.
3. Attach the other bottle using the *Tornado Tube* connector.
4. The spinning action of the vortex removes dirt found on the celery.

Chris reminds us that his vegetable washer does not necessarily remove all of the dirt found on the vegetables. It's a good idea to wash the vegetables again in the sink before eating them.

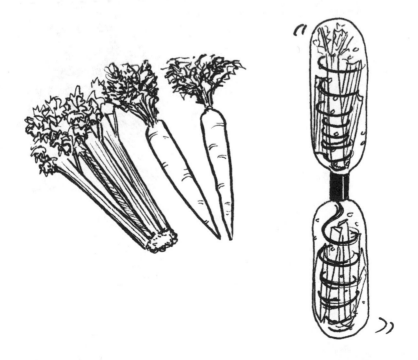

Tornado Tube Straw Dispenser

If you've ever fumbled around the kitchen trying to find a straw or accidentally spilled a whole box of straws in your attempts to remove just one, then Natalie Echter's *Tornado Tube* Straw Dispenser is a must for you. Natalie is a 4th grader at Holy Trinity Elementary. She developed this activity while attending a summer hands-on science camp at Regis University in Denver, Colorado.

Procedure

1. Rinse out a 1 or 2-liter plastic soda bottle using soap and water and allow it to dry completely.
2. Fill the bottle with drinking straws and attach the *Tornado Tube*. Do not attach a second bottle.
3. Turn the bottle upside down and one straw comes out, but the rest of the straws stay inside the bottle.

80

The Perfect Water Balloon Maker

Have you ever had the problem of stretching a balloon over the end of the faucet when you're trying to make a water balloon only to have it slip off and squirt water everywhere? Well, worry no more, because Christopher Echter from Holy Trinity Elementary School used his *Tornado Tube* to invent the *Perfect Water Balloon Maker*.

Procedure

1. Fill a 2-liter plastic soda bottle full of water.
2. Insert the open end of the balloon through the hole in the middle of the *Tornado Tube* and attach the *Tornado Tube* to the bottle. Christopher reminds us that nine inch party balloons work quite well.
3. Attach the *Tornado Tube* to the bottle as shown in the illustration.
4. Turn the bottle upside down and squeeze to fill the balloon with water. Hold onto the neck of the balloon and pull down to release the balloon from the *Tornado Tube*. Tie a knot in the balloon and bombs away!

The Easy Balloon Blower

Since the making of water balloons is not always considered the best indoor activity, you can use the same technique to inflate a balloon with air. Attach the balloon to the *Tornado Tube* as described in the previous activity and blow on the end of the *Tornado Tube* to fill the balloon with air. Hold onto the neck of the balloon and pull down to release the balloon from the *Tornado Tube*.

If you're thinking that this technique is actually more work than blowing up a balloon the old fashion way, you're right. But it's ingenuity that counts, and we want to thank Kate Klock from Shelton Elementary for contributing this activity.

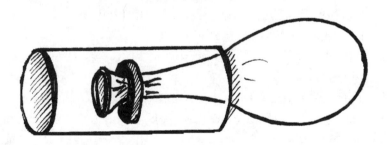

Tornado Tube Hovercraft

Turn the *Easy Balloon Blower* into a *Tornado Tube* Hovercraft in just seconds.

Procedure

1. Carefully cut off the top of a plastic soda bottle using a pair of scissors. Make sure that the rim of the bottle is cut so that it sits perfectly flat on the table.
2. Insert the open end of the balloon through the hole in the middle of the *Tornado Tube*. A nine inch party balloon works well.
3. Blow on the open end of the *Tornado Tube* to inflate the balloon and twist the balloon several times to keep the air from coming out.
4. Attach the *Tornado Tube* to the top of the cut-down soda bottle and set the whole thing on the table as shown.
5. Untwist the balloon and watch as the air from the balloon flows out from under the rim of the bottle. The fast-moving air pushes against the top of the table and causes the hovercraft to glide along the surface.

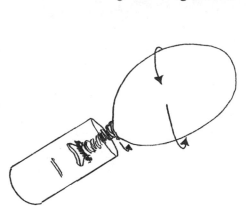

83

The Swimmer's Exercise Tool

Jessica Volz from Wilmore Davis Elementary noticed that some people use empty milk jugs in the swimming pool as exercise floats. Things that float are lighter or less dense than water, and things that sink are heavier or more dense. When the milk jug is filled with air, it floats because the air inside is less dense than the water.

Jessica uses two 2-liter bottles connected with her *Tornado Tube* as another version of the milk jug float. The *Tornado Tube* makes a perfect handle to hold onto the bottles and exercise her arms in the water. Besides, you can make tornadoes in the bottles when you are tired of exercising.

Totally Tubular Voice Disguiser

This activity qualifies as one of the most unusual uses for the *Tornado Tube* that we found. It has nothing to do with tornadoes, a swirling vortex, or even water for that matter. Instead, it explores the science of sound and distorted sound waves.

Procedure

1. Cut a 4 inch square piece of wax paper.
2. Cover one end of the *Tornado Tube* with the wax paper and hold it in place with several twists of a rubber band.
3. Press your lips against the open end of the *Tornado Tube* and speak loudly into the tube. The wax paper resonates from the sound waves of your voice and a very unusual kazoo-like sound comes out of the tube. It's important to speak loudly into the tube and not to blow into the tube. Give it a try!

Big Stream Water Squirter

It's probably not the most practical squirt gun, but it does get the person wet with a big, drenching stream of water. We can thank Alex Wagner and Katie Eilers for this super soaking idea.

Procedure

Fill just one soda bottle to the top with water and attach the *Tornado Tube*. Aim the end of the tube in the appropriate direction and squeeze the bottle with all of your might. The small opening in the middle of the tube restricts the flow of the water just enough to launch a big stream of water.

Derek Giulianelli, a sophomore at Santa Clara University in Santa Clara, California, used this idea late one night when he was annoyed with his roommate's loud snoring. He took apart the *Tornado Tube* experiment that was on his desk and woke up his snoring roommate in a most unforgettable way. The resulting water fight left both roommates completely soaked and a huge mess to clean up.

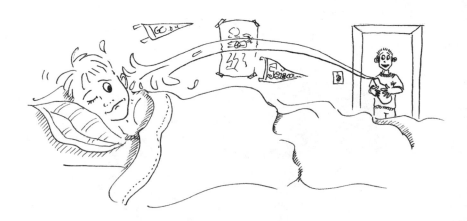

Body Building Barbell

Luming Feng from Maddox Elementary points out that scientists need to exercise both their minds and their muscles. So, in an effort to create a society of muscular scientists, Luming invented the *Tornado Tube* Barbell.

Fill both plastic soda bottles to the top with water. The tricky part is to attach the *Tornado Tube* without spilling too much water. This is best done over the sink or in the bathtub. Position your hand around the *Tornado Tube* and start your workout. Adjust the weight by changing the amount of water in the bottles.

Bubbling Twister

Try adding a few drops of dish detergent to the water in the soda bottles and watch as a bubbling twister appears. Paige Sholar from Dennison Fundamental School, who suggested this idea, also points out that the soap bubbles allow you to see how the water and air exchange places in the bottles.

Procedure

1. Fill the bottle 3/4 full with water.
2. Add 10 drops of dish detergent or liquid soap.
3. Use the *Tornado Tube* to connect the other soda bottle.
4. Shake the water and soap mixture to fill the bottle with bubbles. Swirl the water to start the vortex action. Notice how the soap bubbles are carried down the vortex.
5. Repeat the vortex action several times until both bottles are filled with bubbles. You might need to add a few more drops of soap depending on the hardness of your water.

As water spins down the vortex into the lower bottle, the bubbles that once occupied space in the lower bottle move upward through the middle of the vortex and fill the upper bottle.

Questions: Do the bubbles in the bottles form a common geometric shape? Can you find a honeycomb-shaped bubble structure? Do things like food coloring, sugar, salt, or oil affect the size and shape of the bubbles? The next experiment will provide you with the answers to these questions.

Bubbling Twister II

Before the invention of the *Tornado Tube*, teachers used this recipe to create the illusion of a tornado in a bottle.

Procedure

1. Fill the bottle 3/4 full with water.
2. Add 1 tablespoon of salt.
3. To this mixture add 1 or 2 drops (no more) of soap.
4. Cap the bottle and swirl the liquid quickly in a circular motion and look for the vortex in the middle of the bottle.

The few drops of soap are needed so that the tornado can be seen, and the salt keeps the bubbles small with very little foaming. Use the salt and soap recipe with your *Tornado Tube* and compare the results with the previous experiment.

The Bubbling Twister experiment is featured on the cover of this book. Check it out!

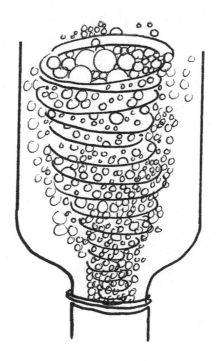

Super Bubble Maker

Cassidy Pangell from All Souls Elementary found a plastic ripple-style straw that fit perfectly into the hole in the middle of the *Tornado Tube*. At first she used the *Tornado Tube* and straw to drink her favorite soda directly from the soda bottle, but then she discovered an even more creative use for their contraption.

Procedure

1. Pour enough water onto a dinner plate to just cover the bottom.
2. Add 15-20 drops of dish detergent and gently stir the mixture.
3. Push just the end of the plastic ripple straw through the hole in the middle of the *Tornado Tube*.
4. Dip the open end of the *Tornado Tube* into the bubble mixture and blow on the straw. Adjust the amount of soap and water needed to make big, beautiful bubbles.

Double-Decker Twister

In June of 1995, Jaymes Adams, Max Mullins, and Casimir Moses-Sommers attended a hands-on science camp for kids at Regis University in Denver, Colorado. The week-long camp was filled with an assortment of mind-bending activities, startling explosions, and slimy concoctions. A portion of the camp was devoted to *Tornado Tube* inventions. While Jaymes, Max, and Casimir all submitted their own separate inventions, we credit all three of them here as inventors of the *Double-Decker Twister*.

Procedure

1. The procedure for building the Double-Decker Twister varies from design to design. This version uses two *Tornado Tube* connectors to join three bottles, Other versions rely on only one *Tornado Tube* and some fancy cutting and gluing of the plastic soda bottles. Regardless of the method, the effect is still the same. Spin the double-decker bottle contraption and create two twisting, twirling tornadoes.

2. Here's one method of making a double-necked bottle. You will need two bottles, scissors, and some silicone glue to assemble the contraption. Silicone glue is available at your local hardware store. If the bottles have a base made out of heavy plastic, remove the base by first filling the bottle with hot water in order to melt the glue.

3. Carefully cut off the top part of one of the bottles as shown in figure 1, and remove the bottom portion of the other bottle as shown in figure 2.

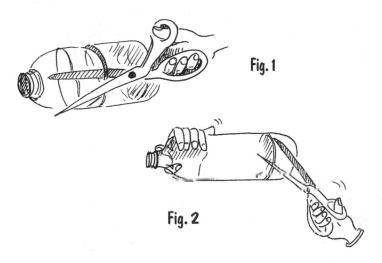

Fig. 1

Fig. 2

4, Place a bead of silicone glue around the rim of the larger bottle, and carefully fit the two pieces together. See figure 3. You may need to work the glue back and forth in order to make a tight seal. Make sure that the bottles are straight before letting the glue dry for at least 24 hours!

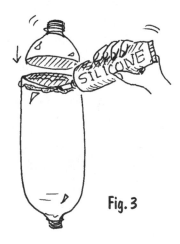

Fig. 3

5. Peel away any excess glue on the outside of the bottle after the glue has completely dried.

6. Fill one of the regular bottles 3/4 full with water. Attach a *Tornado Tube* connector and regular bottle to each end of your double-ended bottle. With a little practice, you'll be swirling twin tornadoes to everyone's amazement.

The parents of the inventors wanted us to remind you that no matter how much glue or tape you use to make this double-decker delight, it sooner or later will begin to leak. Maybe it's a great activity for a hot summer's day...outside.

Jaymes Adams attends school at the Community Involved Charter School, Max Mullins is a student at St. Thomas More, and Casimir Moses-Sommers attends Ellis Elementary.

Sands of Time

If you are a collector of fine time pieces, then you'll want to add this hourglass-like timer to your collection. Craig Burnham, the inventor of the *Tornado Tube*, originally had his mind set on making an hourglass out of old soda bottles, rubber tubing, and hose clamps in his father's cellar. Unfortunately, Craig did not have enough salt to fill the bottles, and the sand around his house was too wet and clumpy to flow between the bottles. So, he substituted water in place of sand or salt and accidentally invented the *Tornado Tube* as we know it today.

Katie Handler from Cheltenham Elementary and Lisa Hesterberg from the Rocky Mountain School for the Gifted and Creative knew nothing of Craig Burnham's original efforts when they suggested their ideas. We applaud their creativity and are pleased to include their experiment in our collection of ideas.

Procedure

1. Fill one of the soda bottles as full as you want with salt or very fine, dry sand.
2. Attach the second bottle using the *Tornado Tube*. Be sure that the second bottle is completely dry.

Turn the bottles upside down so that the sand or salt is on top and you've created an inexpensive hourglass...or maybe it's a minute glass. No need for spinning, swirling, or twirling. Just turn it over and watch.

It's a Tornado Tube Beverage

Megan Grosz from Willow Creek Elementary and Scott McMaster from Crestview Elementary share their culinary skills as they take their *Tornado Tubes* to the kitchen.

Megan uses her *Tornado Tube* to make the perfect chocolate milk. Pour the milk and the appropriate amount of chocolate milk mix into the soda bottle and attach the second bottle using the *Tornado Tube*. No longer are you burdened with the task of stirring milk with something as ordinary and blasé as a spoon. Instead, use the *Tornado Tube* to spin the milk into a swirling vortex to make the perfect glass of dizzy chocolate milk.

Scott, on the other hand, enjoys a tall glass of lemonade with a twist of science. Measure out the correct amount of water and powder mix or fresh-squeezed lemons and sugar. Attach the second bottle and swirl to your heart's content. It's the world's most creative way to make lemonade.

Tornado Tube Bird Feeder

This has to be one of the most unusual
things in the world to do with a
Tornado Tube, and we think it's
great. Alison Nemirow from
Prospect Valley Elementary and
Kelsey Rogers from Maple Grove
Elementary came up with a humanitarian use for the *Tornado
Tube*. Introducing the *Tornado Tube* Bird Feeder.

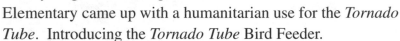

Procedure

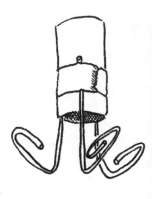

1. You'll need to make a few slight
   modifications to your *Tornado Tube*
   using some paper clips and tape.
   Unfold 3 large paper clips and attach
   them to the *Tornado Tube* as shown in
   the illustration. A strong tape like duct
   tape works well.
2. Carefully poke the paper clips through the center of a small
   plastic plate or aluminum pan. Adjust the pan so that it
   hangs down about one inch from the end of the *Tornado
   Tube*.

3. Bend the paper clips to hold the pan in place.
4. Fill a plastic soda bottle with bird seed, making sure that nothing in the seeds will be too big to fit through the hole in the *Tornado Tube*.
5. Attach the bottle to the *Tornado Tube* and hang the bottle upside down so that the bird seed fills the pan. Use string to hang the bottle in a tree or on the porch.

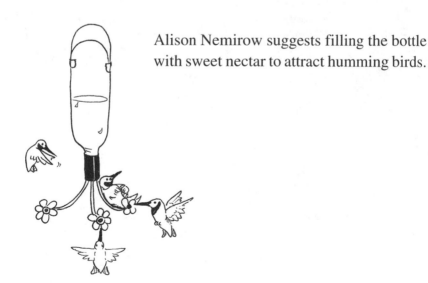

Alison Nemirow suggests filling the bottle with sweet nectar to attract humming birds.

Bowling Pin

Rachel Hodges from Our Lady of Fatima School suggests using two plastic soda bottles and the *Tornado Tube* as a bowling pin. Yes folks...that's right...a bowling pin!

Rachel suggests using ten Tornado Tube connectors and twenty bottles to make a total of ten Tornado Tube bowling pins. Arrange these ten pins in a triangle much like ten pins in a bowling alley. Select a ball that will work well as your bowling ball. The game should be played on a flat surface. When you're tired of bowling you can discuss the science of the vortex action...or you can rest for a second and start bowling again.

It's a *strike* of genius that Rachel had in her *spare* time.

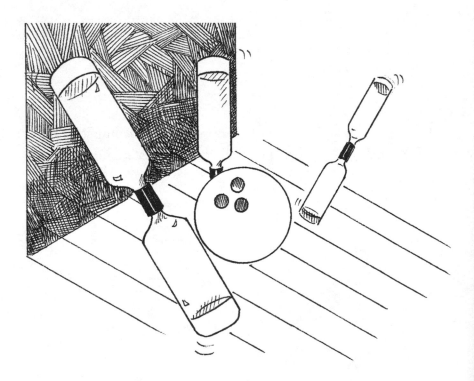

Rainbow Tube

Christy Fabian from Vineland Middle
School developed this really cool way to
show that white light is made from a
spectrum of colors. It's a *Tornado
Tube* spectroscope.

Procedure

1. You'll need to find a small piece of diffraction grating
   measuring approximately one square inch. Diffraction
   grating is a thin piece of plastic with hundreds of
   microscopic lines scratched into the surface. All of the lines
   run parallel to one another and these lines act like a prism.
   As white light passes through the diffraction grating, the
   light is separated into the colors of the rainbow: red, orange,
   yellow, green, blue, indigo, and violet. You can find
   diffraction grating at a hobby store, or you can purchase
   inexpensive prism glasses from your local toy store and
   remove the plastic lenses.

2. Cut the diffraction grating so that it fits inside the *Tornado
   Tube* as shown.

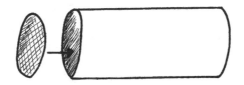

3. Many plastic soda bottles have an opaque bowl-shaped bottom piece that is glued onto the clear plastic bottle. Remove the bottom piece from a plastic soda bottle or select a bottle that does not have a bowl-shaped bottom piece.

4. Cover the bottle in aluminum foil so that no light can leak into the bottle.

5. Cut a small slit (about one inch long) in the aluminum foil on the bottom of the bottle so that just a concentrated ray of light comes into the bottle.

6. Attach the *Tornado Tube* to the bottle, being careful to keep the diffraction grating in place.

7. Put your eye up to the open end of the *Tornado Tube* and point the slit in the aluminum foil into the light. Light that passes through the slit is refracted by the diffraction grating and this creates the spectrum of colors.

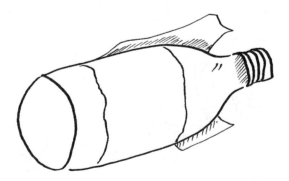

Butterology

The *Tornado Tube* has been used to perform some pretty unusual tasks like cleaning vegetables, dispensing straws, and filling water balloons, but this idea took us all by surprise.

I met Aaron Schultz from Littleton, Colorado, at the summer science camp at Regis University in 1996. He showed up at camp one day with his *Tornado Tube* bottles filled with what looked like thick milk. He explained that the liquid was actually cream. Of course, my next question was, "Why?"

Aaron predicted that the spinning, churning action of the vortex in the bottles would eventually turn the cream into butter. Only time would tell, and a long time it was. Aaron kept swirling the cream for several hours. That's true dedication to your work.

The moment of truth came, and Aaron opened the bottles... Behold, there was butter! At least I think it was butter?

"Scope and Sequins"

A very funny man by the name of Dr. Earl Reum from Denver, Colorado, sent me a *Tornado Tube* contraption for professional educators only. The reason for this is because teachers are the only people who will appreciate this unusual sense of humor. Dr. Reum is a nationally-known speaker in the field of education and student activities, and is the master of the pun.

Earl taped a *Scope* mouthwash label onto one of the bottles and filled it with green colored water to give the appearance of mouthwash in the bottle. He also sprinkled a number of brightly colored sequins in the bottle. Attach the other bottle using the *Tornado Tube* connector and you're ready to go.

Give the mixture a swirl in front of the audience of teachers before you begin talking about the frenzy of activity that surrounds our *Scope and Sequence* policies.

If you don't understand the joke, share it with a teacher friend and look for the smile on his or her face.

Liquid Light

Chemical light sticks have become quite popular over the years, especially around Halloween. In order to make the light stick glow, bend it just enough to break a delicate glass ampule that contains a special chemical. This allows the liquid in the tube and the glass ampule to mix and the resulting chemical reaction gives off energy in the form of light. Light sticks do not create heat or sparks when lit and are completely waterproof.

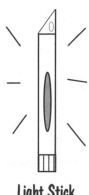

Light Stick

Place a chemical light stick in your favorite *Tornado Tube* bottle to give the water a spooky glow. Some light sticks are small enough to actually get caught up in the vortex. It even makes a great table centerpiece at your next Halloween party.

Raisin' Standards of Excellence

Open a new bottle of *7-Up* or *Sprite* and drop five or six raisins into the soda. Attach an empty bottle with a *Tornado Tube* connector and give it a swirl. You might expect the raisins to spin around the vortex, but there's more...

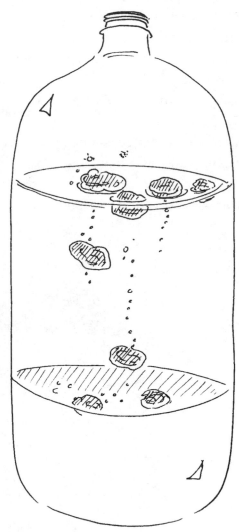

Let the bottle sit undisturbed on the table for a few moments and watch the raisins. As carbon dioxide gas bubbles accumulate on the skin of the raisin, the raisin will become more buoyant and float to the top of the bottle. At the top, the bubbles will burst, and the raisins fall to the bottom of the bottle ready to repeat the cycle. It's the dancing raisins in a *Tornado Tube* bottle full of soda.

When someone inquires as to what you are doing, simply say, "I'm raisin' standards of excellence!" Be careful...you might be accused of raisin' cane.

Tornado Tube Temperature Challenge

How are molecules of hot water and cold water different? In this experiment, you'll use the *Tornado Tube* to make a densimeter, an instrument used to demonstrate the density differences in hot and cold water.

Procedure

1. Place a few drops of food coloring in one of the plastic soda bottles and fill it to the brim with hot water from the faucet.
2. Fill a second plastic soda bottle of equal size to the brim with cold, clear water.
3. Attach the Tornado Tube connector to the bottle with the cold water. Carefully turn this bottle upside down and attach it to the bottle with the hot water. This step is best done in the sink since there will be some leakage when you are connecting the two bottles.
4. Watch closely as the colored, hot water rises up and through the clear, cold water. In turn, the cold water sinks into the bottom bottle. Why?
5. Repeat the experiment, but this time position the hot water on the top and the cold water on the bottom. What differences do you observe?

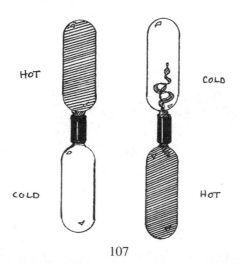

107

Explanation

Imagine a giant hot air balloon and think about what makes it float. The balloon is filled with hot air, and you probably learned that hot air rises. If you sit down on the floor in front of the refrigerator, you'll experience another property of air: cold air is heavier than hot air and it sinks to the ground.

This same phenomenon holds true for hot and cold water. Hot water rises, and cold water sinks. The scientific explanation for this is that the cold water molecules are more dense or closely packed than the hot water molecules. When the bottle with the hot water is on the bottom, the colored liquid rises to the top bottle and the cold, clear water sinks to the bottom bottle. When the hot water is on the top and the cold water is on the bottom, very little mixing of the two liquids occurs.

Meteorologists call this phenomenon *temperature inversion*. Pollution levels can get dangerously high in the winter months in some parts of the country when a layer of cold air is trapped overhead by a layer of hot air. Just as the two liquids did not mix under these circumstances, the two layers of air do not mix and gases like carbon monoxide are trapped in the cold layer of air.

Now It's Your Turn

You might be inclined to turn to this page and say, "That's It!" But there's more.

Now it's your turn to come up with a new use for the *Tornado Tube*. There are hundreds and hundreds of other science experiments and creative activities just waiting to be discovered by someone like you. The weird experiments and wacky ideas that you discovered in this book were contributed by people like you who were experimenting with their *Tornado Tubes* and uncovered a great idea.

They say that most people learn best by doing. You don't become a better soccer player by sitting on the sidelines and only watching the game. You have to get involved and play the game to become the best player you can be. Likewise, to be a great piano player you have to spend hours and hours practicing. It's no different when it comes to learning science. Scientists spend endless hours researching and exploring things that cause them to wonder. Indeed, science is all about wonder, discovery, asking questions, and the excitement of exploration.

I invite you to put on your scientific thinking cap and come up with your own weird and wacky things to do with a *Tornado Tube*. Use the layout on the following page to organize your thoughts and share your ideas with your teachers and friends. Maybe you would like to submit your idea to be considered for the next volume of *Taming the Tornado Tube*.

Send your ideas and experiments to...

Tornado Tube Inventions
WREN Publishing
3145 West Monmouth Avenue
Englewood, Colorado 80110

Invention Name: _____

(Include an introduction and description of your invention.)

Procedure

(What steps are needed to make your invention?)

1.
2.
3.
4.
5.

Collecting Data

(Does your experiment require the reader to collect and analyze data?)

Explanation

(Explain how your invention works and the science of why it works, if necessary)

Draw a Picture of Your Invention

(Include a detailed picture of your invention to help the reader better understand your special design.)

Name of the Inventor: _____

Name of your School: _____

Address: _____

City, State Zip: _____

Chapter 6

Tornado Tube
Theater

Tornado Tube Theater

By now you can see there are literally hundreds of activities, scientific experiments, and off-the-wall things you can do with a *Tornado Tube*. When the creativity in each one of us is unleashed, amazing things happen. There's just one more idea that you need to experience.

In 1993, I had the wonderful opportunity to meet an outstanding teacher from the Fairfax County Public Schools in Fairfax, Virginia. Her name is Bekye Dewey, and in 1987 she was awarded the Presidential Award for Excellence in Science Teaching. Bekye and I often share teaching ideas, manuscripts, and articles, and I asked her to test out a few of the *Tornado Tube* experiments and activities with her students and share with me what happened.

Well, it's not like Bekye to sit at her desk and merely read about science. Bekye is a "doer!" She has a contagious enthusiasm for learning and believes that people learn best by doing. After reading through the activities, Bekye put her creativity to work and developed a skit based on the science of the *Tornado Tube*. It's called the *Wizard of Woeful Weather.* Bekye shares the following script in hopes that it inspires other teachers or students to discover the excitement of participatory science theater.

Preparation Notes:

Nothing in nature inspires such terror as a tornado. It's the heavy weight prize fighter of violent storms. By dramatizing tornado weather, you will get your students or family and friends excited about participating in some hands-on science fun.

Since violent storms are unpredictable, let whimsy be your guide in selecting appropriate clothing for teaching your audience about tornadoes. A white lab coat, unusual safety glasses, and possibly a wild wig might be all that you need to capture the audience's attention.

Don't forget the music. For the stormy ambience, you might use an environmental tape recording of the sounds of a thunderstorm. A more sophisticated *Wizard of Woeful Weather* might play the storms in *The Grand Canyon Suite* by Ferdinand van Grofé.

Scene 1:

Open the classroom door suddenly and walk dramatically into the room. Begin swirling the *Tornado Tube* as you recite slowly the weather chant below:

> *I'm the Wizard of Woeful Weather*
> *Wind and rain I bring together.*
> *Hot air, cold air, boiling black cloud,*
> *Lightning bolts, tornado's shroud.*
>
> *A tornado is a fierce wind storm that becomes a*
> *column of powerful rotating air. When I combine*
> *wind and water in just the right way, a vortex forms.*
> *I'm preparing for the birth of a tornado.*
>
> *I need volunteers to be weather apprentices.*

Distribute several *Tornado Tube* bottles already filled with water to members of the audience.

> *Let's discover how a vortex forms in the Tornado*
> *Tube. Hold the end of the bottle containing the*
> *water upright and begin swirling. How is the water*
> *moving? In what direction does the water move?*
> *Where have you seen water behave like this?*

116

Wait for responses from the audience. Typical responses include: The water is moving in a circle; The water swirls around a column in the center; Water is not flowing in the center of the vortex; Similar behavior is seen as water runs out of the bath tub.

Now, help me to understand what a vortex is.

Develop a definition of a vortex from the responses. For example, a vortex is a rotating column of air or water.

Gravitational attraction for the water pulls the water into the lower bottle. Air from the lower bottle is being pushed up through the opening in the center of the swirling water.

Allow time for the audience to make additional observations before collecting the *Tornado Tube* bottles.

Scene 2:

Bring out from under the table a variety of prepared *Tornado Tube* bottles, each with a different liquid or mixture of liquids. For example, the first bottle is filled with plain water, the second with soap and water, the third with vegetable oil and water, and the last bottle with lemonade. Invite four new volunteers to assist you with the experiment.

Let's have a contest to see who can make the liquid move from the top bottle to the bottom bottle the fastest. When I say go, all of you begin swirling the liquid in your bottles. Members of the audience should watch closely to determine the winner. Ready...get set...go!

What do you see happening in the different bottles? Why do you think this is happening?

Relate the audience's answers to the explanations that are offered with each activity.

Remember that the vortices which you have produced are created by the liquid swirling and being pull downward by gravity. How may the size of the vortex and the length of time it is swirls in the bottle be related to a vortex in a real tornado?

Be sure to allow time for the audience members to talk about what they are observing. It's important to point out that the air in a real tornado is rotating upward!

Scene 3:

Sometimes you may hear a tornado approaching. You may hear a roar like an approaching train or airplane or an unusual buzzing sound.

Use the *Tornado Tube Kazoo* to make the eerie sound. Invite several new volunteers to make a tornado sound with pieces of wax paper and clean *Tornado Tubes*.

How intense a tornado sound can you make? Do you think that the tornado sound you've produced is similar to the sound of a real tornado?

When you've heard just about all of the tornado sounds that you can make, collect the *Tornado Tubes* and the wax paper. Remember to wash the tubes at the end of the activity.

The possibilities are endless! Bekye invites you to finish writing the skit using your favorite activities and experiments in this book. Bring closure to the presentation by asking questions about each of the demonstrations and trying to understand the scientific explanation for things that they observed.

Under the wraps of lab coats, burled in the right brain behind the safety glasses, lies within each of us the ability for acting.

All the world's a stage for science.

-- Bekye Dewey

About the Author

Since 1985, Steve Spangler has captivated more than a quarter of a million students, teachers and parents in schools throughout the country with his science assembly programs, teacher training workshops, and convention seminars. He teaches people of all ages the importance of building connections between educational concepts, hands-on experiences, and real-world applications.

Steve is also becoming a familiar face to television viewers across the country as the science host of *NEWS FOR KIDS*, a nationally syndicated Saturday morning program.

In 1990, Spangler founded WREN Enterprises, Inc. and began producing a line of thought-provoking science toys that are currently being used in more than 2,500 schools nationwide. He is also the author of *Down to a Science*, a three book collection of unique science demonstrations and hands-on activities for educators.

Spangler is currently on staff at Regis University in Denver, acting as the Director of the Regis University *Hands-on Science Institute*, which includes a hands-on training course for teachers combined with a summer science camp for children.

For information on Spangler's speaking programs or his line of hands-on science products, please contact WREN Enterprises, Inc., 3145 West Monmouth Avenue, Englewood, Colorado 80110.

About the Illustrator

Thousands of children in schools throughout the country have visited with Vickie Leigh Krudwig to learn more about the magic of reading, writing, and illustrating.

She published her first illustration when she was just eight years old. Thousands of her illustrations have been published nationally and internationally in a variety of children's publications including *Highlights for Children* and *Kid City Magazine*. Vickie is excited about her upcoming work with the *Children's Television Workshop*.

Vickie is also an active volunteer at area schools. In 1995, she created a publishing program called *Kastle Kids Publishing Company*. This program promotes a hands-on approach to writing, illustrating, and submitting an author's work.

Vickie is a native of Colorado. She lives in Denver with her husband and their three children.